From the Bible-Teaching Ministry of

Charles R. Swindoll

W9-BMQ-413

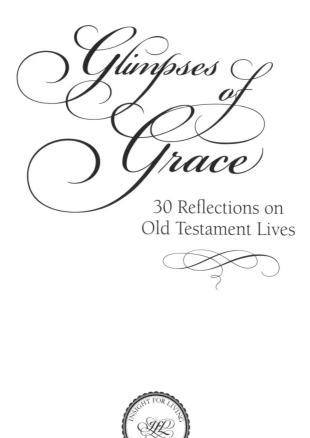

Glimpses of Grace

30 Reflections on
Old Testament Lives

GLIMPSES OF GRACE
30 Reflections on Old Testament Lives
From the Bible-Teaching Ministry of Charles R. Swindoll

Charles R. Swindoll has devoted his life to the accurate, practical teaching and application of God's Word and His grace. A pastor at heart, Chuck has served as senior pastor to congregations in Texas, Massachusetts, and California. Since 1998, he has served as the founder and senior pastor-teacher of Stonebriar Community Church in Frisco, Texas, but Chuck's listening audience extends far beyond a local church body. As a leading program in Christian broadcasting since 1979, *Insight for Living* airs in major Christian radio markets around the world, reaching people groups in languages they can understand. Chuck's extensive writing ministry has also served the body of Christ worldwide and his leadership as president and now chancellor of Dallas Theological Seminary has helped prepare and equip a new generation for ministry. Chuck and Cynthia, his partner in life and ministry, have four grown children, ten grandchildren, and two great-grandchildren.

Copyright © 2013 by Charles R. Swindoll, Inc. and Insight for Living

Published by:
IFL Publishing House
A Division of Insight for Living
Post Office Box 251007
Plano, Texas 75025-1007

Editor in Chief: Cynthia Swindoll, President, Insight for Living
Executive Vice President: Wayne Stiles, Th.M., D.Min., Dallas Theological Seminary
Writers:
    Charles R. Swindoll, C.Th., Dallas Theological Seminary, D.D., L.H.D., LL.D., Litt.D.
    John Adair, Th.M., Ph.D., Dallas Theological Seminary
    Terry Boyle, Th.M., Ph.D., Dallas Theological Seminary
    Jim Craft, M.A., English, Mississippi College
    Heather A. Goodman, Th.M., Dallas Theological Seminary
    Kimberlee Hertzer, M.A., Christian Education, Dallas Theological Seminary
    Andrea Hitefield, M.A., Media and Communications, Dallas Theological Seminary
    Brian Leicht, Th.M., Dallas Theological Seminary
    Malia Rodriguez, Th.M., Dallas Theological Seminary
    Wayne Stiles, Th.M., D.Min., Dallas Theological Seminary
    Colleen Swindoll Thompson, B.A., Communication, Trinity International University
Theological Editors: John Adair, Th.M., Ph.D., Dallas Theological Seminary
    Wayne Stiles, Th.M., D.Min., Dallas Theological Seminary
Content Editor: Kathryn Merritt, M.A., English, Hardin-Simmons University
Copy Editors: Jim Craft, M.A., English, Mississippi College
    Paula McCoy, B.A., English, Texas A&M University-Commerce
Project Coordinator, Creative Ministries: Noelle Caple, M.A., Christian Education,
    Dallas Theological Seminary
Project Coordinator, Publishing: Melissa Cleghorn, B.A., University of North Texas
Proofreader: Paula McCoy, B.A., English, Texas A&M University-Commerce
Art Director: Mike Beitler, B.F.A., Graphic Design, Abilene Christian University
Designer: Laura Dubroc, B.F.A., Advertising Design, University of Louisiana at Lafayette
Production Artist: Nancy Gustine, B.F.A., Advertising Art, University of North Texas

Unless otherwise identified, Scripture quotations are from the *New American Standard Bible*® (*NASB*). Copyright © 1960, 1962, 1963, 1968, 1971, 1972, 1973, 1975, 1977, 1995 by The Lockman Foundation, La Habra, California. All rights reserved. Used by permission. (www.lockman.org)

Scripture quotation marked (MSG) is from *The Message*. Copyright © 1993, 1994, 1995, 1996, 2000, 2001, 2002 by Eugene H. Peterson. All rights reserved. Used by permission of NavPress Publishing Group.

An effort has been made to locate sources and obtain permission where necessary for the quotations used in this book. In the event of any unintentional omission, a modification will gladly be incorporated in future printings.

ISBN: 978-1-57972-988-2
Printed in the United States of America

Table of Contents

A Note from
Chuck Swindoll

When it comes to grace, the Old Testament gets a bad rap. In today's popular mind-set, people see the first half of the Bible as little more than a collection of freedom-denying laws and compassion-challenged commands. Those who speak so loudly against the Old Testament chirp about the excessive regulations on every aspect of life, right down to the threads of clothing. They question God's commands to Israel to wipe out entire populations. They look to the "softer" New Testament for a "better way." And *grace*? Well, that word doesn't come up.

I understand this response . . . at least to a point. The events and laws of the Old Testament do pose some difficult and important questions that need addressing. However, when we leave grace out of our account, we do so at our own peril . . . because grace flows through the Old Testament from beginning to end.

To show grace is to extend favor or kindness to one who doesn't deserve it, can never earn it, and can never repay it. God provided His grace in abundance time and again in the Old Testament. At the moment of creation . . . grace. With Noah in the ark . . . grace. On the dry land in the middle of the parted Red Sea . . . grace. What happened when God granted the Promised Land to His people? Grace. And when He brought them out of exile and back to the land? Grace! Time and time again, God made His grace known in the lives of the people of the Old Testament. Why? Because grace is fundamental to the way He deals with humanity. It always has been, and it always will be.

This little volume put together by our staff at Insight for Living Ministries, *Glimpses of Grace: 30 Reflections on Old Testament Lives*, uses the Old Testament as a canvas to paint a portrait of God's grace through history. The grace you'll see on display here affirms God's good gift of grace in the lives of the well-knowns and the lesser-knowns. As you read, you'll see examples of both vertical grace—God's grace to people—and horizontal grace—people's grace to each other. I love it, and so will you!

We who believe in Jesus Christ as Lord and Savior do so because of grace. And as people of grace, we want to exhibit grace in every aspect of our lives. May this collection of devotional readings enhance your appreciation for the long heritage of grace that has come before us. And may it inspire you to practice grace and look for it from God even more in your life today.

Chuck Swindoll

Charles R. Swindoll

Glimpses of Grace

30 Reflections on Old Testament Lives

*F*or whatever was written in earlier times was written for our instruction, so that through perseverance and the encouragement of the Scriptures we might have hope.

~ Romans 15:4

Then the LORD God formed man of dust from the ground, and breathed into his nostrils the breath of life; and man became a living being.

~ Genesis 2:7

Adam

Receiving the Breath of Life

In the barren stillness of the newly created earth, the Creator drew near to completing the pinnacle of His creation. Gathering dust from the ground, God formed the body of Adam, the first man. Supple skin, two-legged movement, and an astounding capacity for learning ensured that this creature would stand above all others on earth. Into that majestic body, God breathed the breath of life, animating its limbs and bringing expression to its face. Without that breath, the newly formed man would have sat unmoving, an eternal curio rather than a relational creature.

A foundational act of God, the creation of humanity stands as one of the most significant and evident acts of God's grace in all of history. For Adam, the simple fact of his existence announced that God gave him life. The delicate features of Adam's body, the smooth sounds of his breath, and even the unforgiving grit of dust in his hands and feet all served as potent reminders of God's gracious gift of life.

In creation, God communicated His grace in a most tangible and unmistakable fashion. Adam, though alone in the garden, could not miss grace, even if the word had not yet been spoken on earth. As God filled out His creation, the evidence of grace in Eden surrounded Adam: flowering plants, lush trees, beasts of all kinds, and especially Eve—Adam's wife, his companion for life (Genesis 2:24). None of these evidences disappeared when Adam ate from the forbidden tree (3:6).

God's grace continued to shine even as Adam forgot it, choosing instead to take what he wanted and fulfill his own desires. Adam's rejection of grace introduced death into God's good world. Though God graciously extended Adam's life beyond that fateful decision to eat, the destructive effects of Adam's rejection continue today. But so do the tangible evidences and reminders of grace.

Dust, body, and breath were present at the beginning. They are present today. We can still find the dust of the earth—God's material for the creation of humanity—within seconds of looking for it no matter where we find ourselves. We cannot be awake without noticing our bodies. Whether we consider their glorious potential, use them for all manner of work and pleasure, or admire their ingenious construction, our bodies testify to God's matchless grace. And as night falls and the glories of the created world fade to black, we can still hear the rhythms of our breath. Inhale. Exhale. The grace of God moves into and out of us at every moment, waking or sleeping.

~John Adair

THE REST OF THE STORY: Read Genesis 1:1–3:24.

What do you see in the world around you that testifies to God's grace? How does Adam's story enhance your appreciation of grace in everyday life?

But God remembered Noah and all the beasts and all the cattle that were with him in the ark; and God caused a wind to pass over the earth, and the water subsided.

~Genesis 8:1

Noah

Belonging to God

Chaotic waters swarmed the earth in an act of de-creation.

Humans had filled creation with death and destruction. Like Eve, they had seen the forbidden as good and took it. God had seen their true nature, and it grieved Him. Their sin had consequences. They had ruined themselves and all of creation, so God ruined them with judgment.

But He did not abandon creation.

He provided an escape. He chose Noah as His vehicle of grace to rescue not only Noah and his family but all of the animals.

At the center of Noah's story rests God's fulfilled promise. Dry land emerged. Vegetation, animals, and humans repopulated the earth. God restored and blessed humanity once again.

Noah's godliness contrasted the evil and corruption that pervaded the rest of humanity, not because he was perfect but because he had a proper relationship with God. Noah belonged to God. After judgment, God began a new order with His righteous recipients of grace. "Be fruitful and multiply," He repeated, admonishing them to remember the sanctity of life (Genesis 9:1).

As in the creation story, rest followed God's work. He rested from His judgment, and Noah rested in God's covenant. Noah responded to God's offer of grace and redemption with obedience and sacrifice by building the ark. And when God put Noah's feet back on dry land, Noah responded with worship.

But just as Adam fell into shameful nakedness, so Noah fell into shameful nakedness after God's practical re-creation, and the world again entered a downward spiral.

Even the best of the best fail. Humanity cannot save itself. In Noah's day, God responded to the destruction caused by sin with destruction by His judgment, and He will again in the final judgment.

But God will not abandon His creation.

Noah's obedient and sacrificial act pointed toward that of another who will more perfectly, fully, and eternally save believing humanity—Jesus Christ, God's ultimate vehicle of grace. Through Jesus's sacrifice, God will rescue His saints and all of creation from the inclination toward evil. Water washed the earth clean in Noah's day, and new birth in the Holy Spirit washes us clean. Noah was saved through water in the midst of death and re-creation, and we are saved through what baptism represents—a pledge of our identity with Christ's death and resurrection (1 Peter 3:20–21).

After pronouncing His judgment to Noah, God delayed the chaotic floods for 120 years, and He delays His judgment now. Christians can rest in His promise. We believe in "the resurrection of the body and life everlasting." We believe in the ultimate re-creation. As Noah did, we cling to our hope in God with tenacious obedience and sacrifice in a violent and corrupt world, for we belong to God.

~Heather A. Goodman

THE REST OF THE STORY: Read Genesis 6:1–9:29.

How does knowing you belong to God affect how you respond to the evil, injustice, and corruptness in the world around you? How can you share hope with others in your life who need to be rescued?

[God] said, "Take now your son, your only son, whom you love, Isaac, and go to the land of Moriah, and offer him there as a burnt offering on one of the mountains of which I will tell you."

~ Genesis 22:2

Abraham

Letting Go of What We Most Adore

As an aged father, Abraham took increasing delight in his long-awaited son, Isaac—a child of God's grace, born to Abraham and Sarah well past their childbearing years. How precious he was to them! Then one day, in the middle of their delight, the Lord stepped in and commanded the kind, gentle, and aging father to put his only son to death on an altar.

Pause. Ponder. Try to imagine hearing that command.

We can't help but be impressed with Abraham's swift obedience. There was no delay, no hesitation, no bargaining, no arguing, not even a hint of reluctance. Surely, the internal anguish Abraham endured must have been overwhelming . . . but his actions displayed absolute resignation. He and Isaac rose early, prepared the supplies, and started the three-day journey to the region of Moriah, where the Lord told Abraham to go.

Once they arrived, Abraham and Isaac started up the hill God designated. Once they arrived, the father bound his son, laid him on the altar, and raised the knife to bring it down into his son's chest or to swipe it across his throat. This was faith in the wild where the stakes were incredibly high—life and death!

At the last possible moment, God suddenly intervened (Genesis 22:11–12). Stopping Abraham's hand mid-plunge,

God said in effect, "Your willingness to give up your only son has demonstrated that while you love the gift, you love the Giver more." Abraham trusted God. He knew Him to be gracious, both in giving and in taking.

That was then . . . this is now. That was Abraham . . . what about you? What is it you are gripping too tightly? A possession? A dream? A relationship? Your vocation? Perhaps even your child?

Whatever it is, remember that the Lord gave it to you in His grace, and He may now, in His grace, be in the process of taking it away for reasons unknown to you. Is He gently tugging on it? If so, He could be giving you the opportunity to release your grip. If you resist, He may eventually have to pry your fingers away, and it *will* hurt. Don't wait for that to happen. Voluntarily release it.

Ultimately, the decision to hold anything loosely — especially a relationship — is an act of faith in response to God's grace. Human instinct would have us clutch the things we adore most. Releasing them and presenting them to God requires that we trust Him.

~ Charles R. Swindoll

THE REST OF THE STORY: Read Genesis 22:1–19.

Do you adore the gifts more than the Giver? Have you begun to worship the relationships God has granted you rather than the One who gave you those delights?

"What is the matter with you, Hagar? Do not fear, for God has heard the voice of the lad where he is. Arise, lift up the lad, and hold him by the hand, for I will make a great nation of him."

~ Genesis 21:17–18

Hagar

Quenching Your Thirst in a Barren Land

Like a flower wilting under the scorching sun, Hagar felt her life slowly withering away. After giving her son the last sip of water, she did the only thing she felt she could: she left him under a bush and walked away so she wouldn't have to see him die.

This single mother couldn't help but wonder whether or not her son's name was really true. His name, "Ishmael," means, "God hears." *But does God hear? Does God even care?*

After all, Abraham, the father of her only son, had sent them away with only bread and a skin of water. For days, they had "wandered around in the wilderness of Beersheba" (Genesis 21:14), leaving her feeling as dry and empty as the barren wasteland that surrounded her.

As she searched the horizon for any sign of water, the image of Abraham's wife, Sarah, came to Hagar's mind and filled her with regret. True, Hagar had "despised" Sarah, and Ishmael had "mocked" Isaac, but surely they did not deserve such cruel treatment—death from hunger and thirst in a barren land!

Finally—in what she assumed was her last moment to live—Hagar lifted up her voice and cried out to the Lord, "Do not let me see the boy die" (21:16). When all hope seemed lost, *God heard her* and the angel of God spoke to her:

"What is the matter with you, Hagar? Do not fear, for *God has heard* the voice of the lad where he is. Arise, lift up the lad, and hold him by the hand, for I will make a great nation of him." (21:17–18, emphasis added).

In Hagar's time of need, God extended grace. He opened her eyes and revealed what she had so desperately needed—water! God's grace transformed Hagar's life from tragedy to triumph and allowed Ishmael to become the patriarch of a vast nation.

Do you have a troubled past? Have you wandered in the wilderness like Hagar? Don't despair. God's grace is sufficient to transform your past into a future filled with hope. All that is required is for you to turn to Christ. He is the cool cup of water that your thirsty soul longs for. And His invitation extends to each person—young or old, great or small, rich or poor. The words of Jesus still ring true today: "If anyone is thirsty, let him come to Me and drink. He who believes in me, as Scripture said, 'From his innermost being will flow rivers of living water'" (John 7:37–38). Call out to the Lord. *He will hear you.*

~ *Kimberlee Hertzer*

THE REST OF THE STORY: Read Genesis 21:8–21.

How does Hagar's account help you understand God's grace in your life? Have you cried out to God to meet your needs?

_____

_____

_____

_____

_____

_____

_____

_____

_____

_____

_____

_____

_____

_____

_____

_____

_____

_____

"Deliver me, I pray, from the hand of my brother, from the hand of Esau; for I fear him, that he will come and attack me and the mothers with the children."

Jacob and Esau

Facing the Fear of Dependency on God

Bitter betrayals produce persistent wounds. Conflict hardens hearts into fortresses of resentment.

The schemes of Jacob ("the deceiver") loaded his brother, Esau, with resentment. In case we're tempted to think Esau innocent, remember what the Bible tells us. Esau was indifferent to the plans of God. "Immoral . . . godless . . . he found no place for repentance, though he sought for it with tears" (Hebrews 12:16–17).

From Esau's perspective, the blessing of his father, and even God's favor, had been stolen. Esau marched up from Seir with four hundred men.

Hearing of Esau's approach, Jacob panicked, calling on all his old deceitful tricks. Jacob was used to making it in life . . . without God. Jacob's maneuvering is demonstrated in three steps.

First, Jacob arranged his people and his herds into two groups to make his escape from Esau. (Step one: "Save myself.") Jacob then reminded God that God had gotten him into this mess and that God's integrity was on the line. (Step two: "Say a quick prayer in case the Lord can do me some good.") Finally, Jacob sent his family away and lavished Esau with gifts. (Step three: "Cover up past offenses with flattery and good will.")

Once Jacob exhausted every self-protective strategy, he "was left alone" (Genesis 32:24).

Trapped by the fruit of his own deceit and facing death, the deceiver Jacob met the Lord.

Have you noticed that our greatest fear is often putting ourselves in the hands of God when it really matters? All his life, Jacob had wrestled against his fathers' God. Then, Jacob met God in hand-to-hand combat, tangling all night until they were locked in a surreal stalemate. Finally, with surgical precision, the Lord touched Jacob's strongest joint, and POW!—he was dealt a crippling blow.

Weak and disabled, Jacob confronted his greatest fear on the wide open plain of uncertainty. In faithfulness, God intervened and granted favor. Lifesaving reconciliation came from heaven to these famously feuding brothers. Not only did Jacob live, but "Esau ran to meet him and embraced him, and fell on his neck and kissed him, and they wept" (33:4).

By the grace of God, the fortified walls of their hearts crumbled. The brothers made peace in a miraculous embrace. God gave Jacob the name Israel, "the one who strives." And Jacob no longer held God at a distance as the God of his fathers. He knew God by a new name, "the God of Israel," *his* God.

~Brian Leicht

THE REST OF THE STORY: Read Genesis 32–33.

Have you ever wrestled with God to assert your independence from Him? How has God touched you (POW!) to reveal your inability when you faced impossible circumstances, fear, or conflict? How does He show His grace through our weakness?

"Now do not be grieved or angry with yourselves, because you sold me here, for God sent me before you to preserve life. . . . God sent me before you to preserve for you a remnant in the earth, and to keep you alive by a great deliverance. Now, therefore, it was not you who sent me here, but God."

~ Genesis 45:5, 7–8

Joseph

Factoring God's Sovereignty into Our Pain

Joseph's brothers had done him wrong, and now, he had the power to get even . . . in spades! Humanly speaking, the average individual, when faced with people who have "done us wrong," would likely frown and demand, "You think you know what humiliation is all about. You wait until I'm through with you. I've been waiting all these torturous years for this moment!" But not Joseph. He was a changed man. He was God's man, which means he was a great man. And so, many long years after his brothers sold him into slavery, Joseph looked into their anxious eyes and with the arm of the Lord supporting him said in all sincerity, "It was not you who sent me here, but God."

Years later, Joseph said this once more to his brothers who were still worried. Though a long time had passed since Joseph extended them grace in Egypt, they still worried about what he might do to them after their father's death.

Guilt clings to the side of the boat, clawing for a foothold, long after grace has come onboard and begun to steer. That's why Joseph repeated his gracious words: "As for you, you meant evil against me, but God meant it for good in order to bring about this present result, to preserve many people alive" (Genesis 50:20). How magnanimous of Joseph! What a magnificent, God-directed attitude!

Think about what goes on inside your skin, the memories that haunt you, or the pain you live with because of someone's wrongdoing. Each of us, at one time or another, has been treated badly. When that happens, your perspective becomes cloudy. You remember the manipulation. You remember the wrong. You remember the unfair treatment. You remember the torturous trauma, the rejection. Evil was done to you. It was *meant* to be evil! This is no time to deny it—the person deliberately hurt you.

Joseph said to his brothers, "You meant it for evil." He wasn't living in denial. There was nothing good in their motives—and he said so. "But God"! Here is where Joseph allowed his theology to eclipse his human emotions and bad memories—an excellent tradeoff.

Attitude is crucial in the life of the Christian. We can go through Sunday motions, we can carry out religious exercises, we can pack Bibles under our arms and sing songs from memory, yet all the while we can hold grudges against the people who have wronged us. In our own way—perhaps even with a little religious manipulation—we'll get back at them.

But that is not God's way. In Joseph, God showed us the right way. He gave us an example of a great man—someone supportive, merciful, gracious, generous, and forgiving.

~ *Charles R. Swindoll*

THE REST OF THE STORY: Read Genesis 45 and 50.

The Lord had Joseph's story recorded in sacred Scripture for a reason. How do Joseph's words help dislodge the grudge you have against a person who hurt you? What happens when you factor God's sovereignty into your past pain?

_____

_____

_____

_____

_____

_____

_____

_____

_____

_____

_____

_____

_____

_____

_____

_____

Moses and Aaron gathered the assembly before the rock. And he said to them, "Listen now, you rebels; shall we bring forth water for you out of this rock?" Then Moses lifted up his hand and struck the rock twice with his rod.

~ Numbers 20:10–11

Moses

Living with the Consequences

Moses was bitterly angry with all the complainers he had to lead. It had gone on so long, he was at his wits' end. So in spite of God's command to speak to the rock, Moses deviated to his own loss of temper and let the people have it with a verbal onslaught (Numbers 20:10). Where did he get the okay to deliver such a scathing address? The truth is, he didn't. Then where did it come from? Anger. Moses's short fuse prompted him to take advantage of an opportunity to level those *rebels* with simmering verbiage.

A hint of blasphemy lurked in his words: "Shall *we* bring water out of the rock?" (emphasis added). We? That prompts us to ask, *But Moses, when did you ever bring water out of a rock? Isn't God the one who summons water?* But when we give in to rage, we set aside our right minds as we are driven by our unchecked emotions.

God told Moses to *speak* to the rock. Moses *struck* it, not just once but twice. It's doubtful he even cared if water came. Perhaps he was so angry he wanted their throats to stay dry. He may have thought, *You think we'll give you water, you low-life scumbags? Hah!*

So he belted the rock—Wham! Wham!—and to his surprise, out came water abundantly. Absolutely amazing! Amazing *grace*!

But that's the way God's grace works. You and I have acted in rash unbelief, and God went ahead and opened the door *in spite of us*! Talk about humiliation! It happens when we're out-to-lunch spiritually, when we're walking in the flesh and we know it. We knew the depth of our carnality from the get-go, but God graciously gave us what was best anyway.

It's remarkable, isn't it, this thing called grace? Grace brought forth that clear stream of fresh water in spite of the Israelites' whining rebellion and Moses's wild temper. But don't think for a moment that God excused Moses's tantrum. God couldn't. Therefore, He didn't. God told His servant flatly that as a consequence, he would not step foot into the Promised Land (Numbers 20:12).

But didn't God forgive Moses? Yes, indeed. More to the point, you might be asking, *Won't God forgive me if I disobey?* Yes, He will. But let's suppose you commit a sin frequently (as in Moses's case) and your unbroken habit brings reproach upon the name of Christ. God will forgive that sin each time it's honestly confessed, but the earthly consequences of repeated sins can be terribly painful. Sometimes that's what it takes to get us back where we should be.

Is God longsuffering? You know He is. But He won't always remain patient. Forgiving? Yes, but there are times even forgiven sins bear terrible consequences. We cannot undo sinful deeds or unsay sinful words, but we *can* learn from them. That's why, along with forgiveness, consequences are part of God's grace.

~*Charles R. Swindoll*

THE REST OF THE STORY: Read Numbers 20.

What significant lessons have you learned from the poor decisions you have made? Did you have to learn some of them more than once?

_____

_____

_____

_____

_____

_____

_____

_____

_____

_____

_____

_____

_____

_____

_____

_____

But the LORD said to Moses, "Put back the rod of Aaron before the testimony to be kept as a sign against the rebels, that you may put an end to their grumblings against Me, so that they will not die."

~ Numbers 17:10

Living Up to God's Choice

Moses's big brother, Aaron, had a problem: he didn't grasp the importance of things. With Moses up on the mountain, it didn't take Aaron long to compliantly help the people run headlong into pagan ways. His explanation is comically pathetic:

> "I said to them, 'Whoever has any gold, let them tear it off.' So they gave it to me, and I threw it into the fire, and out came this calf." (Exodus 32:24)

Moses seethed with fury when he saw the idol, but Aaron couldn't understand. The appointed spokesman seemed to shrug and say, "Calm down, Moses. It just sort of happened." Aaron didn't stand firm against the people's pressure, because he didn't grasp the gravity of the mistake he was making.

Later, Aaron saw his two eldest sons die for angering God with their sloppy approach to their priestly duties. Leviticus 10:8–10 reveals that Aaron subsequently received strict instructions from God not to let *himself or his sons* serve at the altar drunk, so that the holy and the profane would be clearly distinguished. Clearly, the high priest hadn't grasped the solemnity of his own duties, and he certainly hadn't taught his sons the importance of theirs.

Add to this the way in which Aaron joined his sister, Miriam, in her challenge against Moses (Numbers 12). Miriam is named first and bore the brunt of God's punishment, so she was likely the instigator. But Aaron was right behind her, joining in until leprosy humbled Miriam. Only then did Aaron give his actions a second thought. Only then did he realize the foolishness of going along with his sister's arrogance.

But from the beginning, Aaron was chosen by God as a part of the plan to redeem Israel out of Egypt. In spite of Aaron's carelessness and his lack of discernment, God appointed him as Moses's spokesman. And when push came to shove, God was ready to stand by His choice. Push *did* come to shove when Korah, a clan chief from the tribe of Levi, attempted to topple Moses and Aaron from their leadership.

In the aftermath of God's judgment against the rebels, God issued a definitive statement concerning Aaron (Numbers 17). Moses gathered all the staffs of the tribal chieftains. The staffs were symbols of authority, and the staff from Levi bore Aaron's name. That staff budded and produced fruit overnight, validating Aaron's leadership position. And incidentally, the tribe of Levi didn't get their staff back. It remained in the ark of the covenant as a constant reminder that Aaron's authority was never to be challenged again.

Aaron wasn't perfect. In fact, he often acted foolishly! But, thankfully, God's grace has nothing to do with our mistakes. It has everything to do with God's mercy. He chooses us *in spite of* ourselves, not *because of* ourselves.

~ *Terry Boyle*

THE REST OF THE STORY: Read Hebrews 5:1–6; 7:11–17; 9:1–28.

If you feel that you just aren't special enough to serve God, how can Aaron's account encourage you to reconsider? Are you meeting your responsibility to keep the holy and the profane separated?

"For if by now I had put forth My hand and struck you and your people with pestilence, you would then have been cut off from the earth. But, indeed, for this reason I have allowed you to remain, in order to show you My power and in order to proclaim My name through all the earth."

~ Exodus 9:15–16

Pharaoh

Having a Chance to Choose

Picture this. You're the leader of the most formidable nation on earth. You have money, fame, and supernatural status. Your servants are at your beck and call, and the army marches at your command. There's nothing that you can't do or have.

You're the master of your destiny until someone challenges your dominion. Rage swells, and your heart begins the process of petrification.

In ancient Egypt, Pharaoh reigned over the political and religious affairs of the most influential empire in the world. To top it off, his subjects worshiped him as a god. So when Moses spoke on behalf of the one, true God, commanding Pharaoh to release the Israelites, he refused. Like thick fog on a dark night, pride prevented Pharaoh from seeing God and responding to His grace.

God gave Pharaoh several chances to repent, graciously sending signs of His power and delaying His ultimate judgment. Each plague that came to Egypt proved that Yahweh ruled over all "gods" and over Pharaoh. Had Pharaoh obeyed, the Lord would not only have freed the Hebrews from slavery; He would have freed Pharaoh from self-delusion and sin. But Pharaoh didn't recognize God's disastrous plagues as grace. Instead, Pharaoh stiffened his neck.

And God extended grace once more.

As Pharaoh stood at the edge of the Red Sea, he faced one last choice. Had he stopped on the shore and dropped to his knees, we would remember him as a protagonist in the Exodus story. Instead, after God parted the Red Sea for His nation, He closed the waters and flooded the rebellious Egyptian king and his army.

Pharaoh's hard heart shows us that God's grace is more formidable than His enemies. Although Pharaoh refused to bow, God used him to help strengthen the Israelites' faith. The Lord revealed His unmatched power over Pharaoh in order to encourage His people to trust Him, both there at the Red Sea and wherever He led them next. Throughout the centuries, from generation to generation, the account of the Exodus was told and retold. And whenever the Israelites feared their enemies, they could look back at God's supremacy over Pharaoh and stand firm.

Like Pharaoh, we have a choice—to put our faith in the Lord and submit to His plan or to trust in our own abilities. God asked a lot of Pharaoh—to turn his back on his sovereignty, fame, and supernatural status. And God asks us to deny ourselves and follow Him. This gracious command places us smack dab in the middle of His redemptive plan.

Remember: God will accomplish His purposes, whether or not we follow Him. He wants to free us from our self-delusion and sin, but He requires a humble response. Let's choose to see grace when God challenges us to acknowledge Him as Lord . . . and let's respond with humble submission.

~Malia Rodriguez

THE REST OF THE STORY: Read Exodus 7–10.

Has pride blinded you to God's Word and His gracious voice in your life? How will you respond to grace today?

_____

_____

_____

_____

_____

_____

_____

_____

_____

_____

_____

_____

_____

_____

_____

_____

_____

_____

Then they set out from Mount Hor by the way of the Red Sea, to go around the land of Edom; and the people became impatient because of the journey. The people spoke against God and Moses, "Why have you brought us up out of Egypt to die in the wilderness?"

~ Numbers 21:4–5

The Hebrews

Taking the Long Way

The brand-new Hebrew nation began their journey from Egypt to the Promised Land by promptly turning away from it. Rather than heading the Hebrews down the direct coastal route to Canaan, God directed them southeast toward the Red Sea. The direct route led through the land of the Philistines, and while God could have just destroyed the enemy (as He would the Egyptians at the Red Sea), He was more concerned with the unprepared and fearful hearts of His people (Exodus 13:17).

God had yet to give the people His Word at Mount Sinai, and they didn't yet have the heart to obey it. God's deliverance by parting the Red Sea paved the way for the Hebrews to meet God face-to-face at Sinai—and to receive the Law by which they could live in the Promised Land.

If the goal had simply been a destination, God would have seemed a poor travel agent—a journey that could've taken three weeks ultimately took forty years! But God purposed to give His people something far greater than a parcel of land; He offered them changed hearts. The land, the journey to it, and even God's Word along the way came as but the means by which they would learn to know and trust Him.

Finally, when it was time to enter the Promised Land, instead of entering from the south where the people stood, the Lord led them east around Edom. As a result, the people "became impatient because of the journey" (Numbers 21:4). Why take the long way around? The extra miles seemed pointless.

But as the passage unfolds, we read how God gave Israel victories all up and down the King's Highway east of the Jordan River until they ultimately gained control of the majority of Transjordan. This allowed them to prepare to cross over the Jordan River into the Promised Land at a location far more strategic than from the south. The long way ended up the best way after all.

In our lives, it often seems as if God needlessly extends our journey. For years we pray for a loved one's health, a friend's salvation, or a missionary's financial needs. We plug away endlessly at a miserable job with no promotion. The long way seems the wrong way and, like the Hebrews, we become impatient because of the journey.

Yet when we look back in hindsight, we see God's grace in His delays. We come to appreciate how God used the journey—and all the victories and failures along the way—to prepare us for something we felt ready for much earlier but really weren't. While we strain to see over the next horizon, God sees the map from above—and so He always knows the best way to proceed.

~ *Wayne Stiles*

Adapted from Wayne Stiles, *Going Places with God: A Devotional Journey Through the Lands of the Bible* (Ventura, Ca.: Regal Books, 2006), 66, 89.

THE REST OF THE STORY: Read Exodus 13:17–18; Numbers 21:1–5.

Have you ever experienced an occasion when God's mysterious leading proved wiser than your impatient pleas for progress? Now consider your current situation—how might God receive more glory by your trusting Him along the path of the unknown than by your seeing His purposes from the start?

By faith Rahab the harlot did not perish along with those who were disobedient, after she had welcomed the spies in peace.

~ Hebrews 11:31

Rahab

Receiving Grace as an Outsider

Have you ever felt like an outsider—always peering through the window but never allowed inside? That's how Rahab, a harlot living in the city of Jericho, felt. She was a foreigner, a stranger to God's people, though she wanted to become one of them.

Rahab had heard about God's power—how He divided the Red Sea and drowned the Egyptians. She also knew that Yahweh planned to give Canaan to His people by destroying all its current residents—including her! She trusted in the God of Israel. But as an outsider, how could she join God's family?

Rahab lived between the two fortified walls surrounding Jericho. Each morning from her window, she watched people traveling in and out of the city. She looked for the mighty Israelite army and wondered if that day would be her last.

Then one day, God broke down the invisible wall that separated Rahab from His people. How? He sent Israelite spies into Jericho to assess the land, and when they needed shelter, God directed them to Rahab's door. God gave her an opportunity to experience His grace! And Rahab responded with faith, risking the death penalty for treason and demonstrating her trust in the God of Israel by hiding the spies from her king. And God protected her.

As the spies slipped out of the city, they instructed Rahab to hang a scarlet cord from the window she had let them use to escape. The cord would serve as a sign of her faith and would bring protection for her and all who took refuge in her home when the Israelites came. God kept His promise to this outsider—as the conquering army entered Jericho, they noticed the cord hanging from Rahab's window and spared her and her family.

The scarlet cord recalls the first Passover when the angel of death graciously passed over the Israelite homes marked by the blood of a lamb. All of Jericho had likely heard the Passover story and the testimony of Yahweh's power. But while others hardened their hearts as Pharaoh had done, Rahab and her family believed.

And that's not the end of the story. Rahab eventually married Salmon, and they became the great-great grandparents of King David. Matthew 1:5 reminds us that Rahab has an eternal place in the genealogy of the Lord Jesus. That's amazing grace!

Like Rahab, all who believe in God were once outsiders. But through Jesus, God graciously broke down the fortified wall that separated us from Him and His people. "Remember that you were at that time separate from Christ, excluded from the commonwealth of Israel, and strangers to the covenants of promise, having no hope and without God in the world" (Ephesians 2:12). Thank God for His grace, which makes us not only insiders but *members* of His family.

~*Malia Rodriguez*

THE REST OF THE STORY: Read Joshua 2.

How often do you thank God for making you part of His family? How does the biblical account of God's grace in Rahab's life inspire you to reach out to non-Christians?

_____

_____

_____

_____

_____

_____

_____

_____

_____

_____

_____

_____

_____

_____

_____

_____

_____

The LORD said to Gideon, "The people who are with you are too many. . . . Now therefore come, proclaim in the hearing of the people, saying 'Whoever is afraid and trembling, let him return and depart from Mount Gilead.'" So 22,000 people returned, but 10,000 remained.

~Judges 7:2–3

Gideon

Moving from Fear to Faith

We would never learn to trust God if He didn't put us in places that expose our fear and force us to face it. Fear gets uprooted no other way.

For thousands of years, water from the Spring of Harod has flowed from the mouth of a cave at the bottom of Mount Gilboa in Israel. This spring refreshed innumerable travelers throughout centuries. But for Gideon, it provided much more.

There he learned to trust God.

Although God had promised Gideon a great victory, the doubtful judge still requested a sign. And God graciously obliged (Judges 6:36–40). Yet, the assurance of God's promises didn't negate the circumstances that forced Gideon to trust. Gideon's fleece didn't cause 135,000 Midianites to disappear; he still had to trust God for deliverance.

Then, knowing that the Hebrews, though badly outnumbered, would boast in their victory, God told Gideon to bring his men down to the spring and separate them on the basis of how they drank. Thinning the ranks put Gideon in a position in which his fear would be exposed again. Gideon had sought security with the fleece, using it to get confirmation of God's promises. And though God acquiesced, the Lord immediately countered by putting Gideon in an even more precarious position. If he struggled to trust God at 4 to 1 odds, how would he react to 450 to 1?

Some situations today seem as bleak, hopeless, and pointless as Gideon's must have seemed to him. Circumstances and emotions will demand that we doubt what God has clearly promised. But our confidence must remain in what God has said, not in what we see. In His grace, God helps us understand that truth by taking us places to free us from fear and convince us that He can do what He said.

We shouldn't need a sign to confirm what God has already promised, just the faith to follow Him. How grateful we find ourselves when the Father extends grace to us by ignoring our immature pleas for relief and letting us squirm. As we face unavoidable fears, we begin to discover what escape would never have allowed us to learn: God does what He says He will. In these moments, we move from fear to faith.

~ *Wayne Stiles*

Adapted from Wayne Stiles, *Going Places with God: A Devotional Journey Through the Lands of the Bible* (Regal, 2006), 135.

THE REST OF THE STORY: Read Judges 7:1–25.

Do you find yourself in a situation right now where God is exposing your fear? How can you apply faith in spite of the facts?

_____

_____

_____

_____

_____

_____

_____

_____

_____

_____

_____

_____

_____

_____

_____

_____

_____

_____

The neighbor women gave him a name, saying, "A son has been born to Naomi!" So they named him Obed. He is the father of Jesse, the father of David.

~ Ruth 4:17

Naomi

Moving from Bitterness to Blessing

As she packed up her few belongings to make the long journey back home, Naomi felt as though God had abandoned her. She felt alone, even though her daughter-in-law had promised to provide companionship. With each dusty step, bitterness pounded deeper into Naomi's heart. Though she searched, she couldn't find God's grace in her life.

As a wife and mother of two sons, Naomi's life had once looked picture-perfect. But then, at the time of the judges, a famine plagued Israel. Naomi and her family packed up, left their land, and settled in Moab. Just when she thought she had overcome misfortune, her husband, Elimelech, died, leaving her without provision to raise her sons. Naomi must have thought, *Surely the Lord wouldn't allow more disaster into my life*.

But He did.

Next, Naomi's sons died. Alone in a foreign land, Naomi's hope withered, and bitterness took root.

In Naomi's culture, when tragedy marked a person's life, others viewed that person as cursed by God. Naomi no doubt spent long days and sleepless nights analyzing her life, her thoughts, her choices. *What have I done to offend Yahweh?* she must have wondered. But she kept on, moving from Moab back to Israel, with nothing to look forward to but a life of lonely poverty.

Behind the scenes, God was working in Naomi's life. Through fiery trials, the Lord was graciously refining Naomi's character.

But God didn't deliver Naomi from her pain immediately. The road from bitterness to joy is usually a long one, and God never removes His children prematurely from a trial. Why? Because character transformation is God's objective. And that can't happen quickly. Because of grace, God lets our trials last as long as it takes to make us more like Christ.

As the story progressed, Naomi's daughter-in-law, Ruth, embraced Naomi and pledged to provide for her. Each step on their journey revealed God's grace. God led Ruth to Naomi's kinsman-redeemer, Boaz, who married Ruth and with her had a son. And God's grace didn't stop there. Not only did this son restore Naomi's faith, but her future descendant would be the One to restore millions to God. Grace not only introduced hardship to develop Naomi's spiritual muscles; it placed her in the lineage of our Savior. God's grace turned bitterness into blessing.

What trials are you facing? Job loss? A broken relationship? Discouragement? No one is promised a happy ending, but God's grace will enable you to trust Him during difficult times. God wants to refine you, His dear child, and make you more like Jesus. The Lord used suffering to transform Naomi, and He included her in His redemptive plan. He will do the same for you!

~ Malia Rodriguez

THE REST OF THE STORY: Read Ruth 1–4.

What difficulties in your life have tested your trust in God's grace? How does knowing God's purpose for trials—to make you more like Christ and use you in His redemptive plan—change your response to them?

_____

_____

_____

_____

_____

_____

_____

_____

_____

_____

_____

_____

_____

_____

_____

_____

_____

She said, "Let your maidservant find favor in your sight." So the woman went her way and ate, and her face was no longer sad.

~ 1 Samuel 1:18

Hannah and Samuel

Finding Sanctuary from Suffering

Hannah had a Ph.D. in misery.

As a childless woman in a culture that considered infertility the ultimate failure, Hannah endured remarks that hurt worse than lemon juice squeezed onto an open wound. Her husband's other wife had children of her own, and she "taunted [Hannah] cruelly, rubbing it in and never letting her forget that God had not given her children" (1 Samuel 1:6 MSG).

But all that changed one day.

Perhaps she felt it just as soon as she opened the door of the tabernacle at Shiloh—this was the sanctuary her weary soul longed for. Inside, thick curtains separated her from the Most Holy Place, and she could sense the palpable presence of God that hovered above the ark of the covenant. Imagine how emotionally charged her prayer must have been as she wept bitterly before the Lord (1:10)! Eli, the high priest, responded to her cries, promising that God had seen her suffering and would answer her petition (1:17).

In an incredible act of grace, God provided a son for Hannah. Not surprisingly, she called him Samuel, a Hebrew name that means, "name of God," and that shares the same Hebrew consonants as the word for "asked"—for she said, "I have asked him of the LORD" (1:20). After Samuel was weaned,

Hannah brought him back to the temple and dedicated him to the Lord, leaving the boy in the care of Eli.

As Samuel grew, he also was no stranger to God's grace. One night, as Samuel slept just a few feet from the Most Holy Place, he heard a voice. At first, he thought Eli had called him, so he went to see what the priest wanted. But after three times, Eli realized God was speaking to Samuel. So the fourth time Samuel heard the voice, he responded, "Speak, for Your servant is listening" (3:10).

Hannah struggled through barrenness. Samuel endured a painful separation from his mother. Life delivers misery in different ways. Whether we lose a home to foreclosure or we watch a loved one endure a slow death, pain comes to all of us. But like Hannah and Samuel, we each have the promise that although we experience suffering in our lives, God offers hope and an ultimate solution. Only in Him will our weary souls find sanctuary.

Sometimes God will allow a season of lack or even a grievous loss to set the stage for our greater appreciation for His magnificent grace.

~ *Kimberlee Hertzer*

THE REST OF THE STORY: Read 1 Samuel 1:1–28; 3:1–21.

How have you experienced God's grace in the midst of suffering? Have the miseries of your life made God's grace more splendid?

_____

_____

_____

_____

_____

_____

_____

_____

_____

_____

_____

_____

_____

_____

_____

_____

_____

_____

_____

_____

The king said, "Is there not yet anyone of the house of Saul to whom I may show the kindness of God?" And Ziba said to the king, "There is still a son of Jonathan who is crippled in both feet."

~ 2 Samuel 9:3

Reaching to the Undeserving

David's response to learning about Jonathan's living, crippled son, Mephibosheth, is dripping with compassion. David didn't ask, "How badly is he crippled?" He didn't even ask how Mephibosheth happened to be in that condition. David only inquired, "Where is he?" (2 Samuel 9:4).

That's how grace operates. Grace isn't picky. Grace doesn't look for people who have done things to deserve love. Grace goes into action apart from the response or the ability of the individual. Grace is one-sided. Grace is God giving Himself in full acceptance to someone who does not deserve it, can never earn it, and will never be able to repay it. And grace is what makes the story of David and Mephibosheth so memorable. A strong and famous king stooped down and reached out to one who represented everything David was not!

David, out of sheer love for his deceased friend, Jonathan, demonstrated grace to Jonathan's physically disabled son. David restored Mephibosheth from a place of barrenness to a place of honor. David took this broken, disabled person from a hiding place where there was no pastureland and brought him to the place of plenty, right into the very courtroom of the king.

The analogy is clear. God, out of love for His Son, Jesus Christ, accepts the penalty that Jesus paid on the cross for us, demonstrating grace to the believing sinner. God is still seeking people who are spiritually disabled, dead due to depravity, lost in trespasses and sins, hiding from God—broken, fearful, and confused people. Those of us who have believed in Jesus are walking with God today because He demonstrated His grace to us out of love for His Son. God has taken us from where we were and brought us to where He is. He has brought us into fellowship with Himself, restoring us to what we once had in Adam.

David adopted Mephibosheth into his family, making him one of the king's sons. This is what God has done for believing sinners. He has adopted us into the family of the heavenly King. He has chosen us and made us a member of His family, saying, "You sit at My table. You enjoy My food. I give you My life." What grace!

~ *Charles R. Swindoll*

THE REST OF THE STORY: Read 2 Samuel 9.

Consider where you were when God "found" you and called you to Himself. What similarities do you see between David and Mephibosheth and Jesus and you?

David said to Abigail, "Blessed be the LORD God of Israel, who sent you this day to meet me, and blessed be your discernment, and blessed be you, who have kept me this day from bloodshed and from avenging myself by my own hand."

~ 1 Samuel 25:32–33

Abigail

Acting as a Person of Grace

David was broken down and brokenhearted.

He had lost his mentor, his wife, and his best friend. Now he hid in the wilderness—a place of desolation—hunted by King Saul. In need of sustenance for himself and his men, David turned to Nabal, a fellow tribesman enjoying a time of celebration. David knew the Law called for Israelites to share with the less fortunate. Furthermore, he had protected Nabal's shepherds. David had every right to the gift he requested.

But Nabal, known for his harsh, unreasonable, and evil ways, responded with rejection and insult.

Encountering hostility where he should have received hospitality, David swore to kill Nabal and all the males of Nabal's household. In the past, David had trusted God in the midst of adverse circumstances, but now he reacted in anger and self-justification.

Into this standoff stepped grace.

With everyone's life on the line, one of David's servants sought help from someone known for her good judgment and wisdom—Nabal's wife, Abigail. She responded with levelheadedness and obedience by sharing generously and by serving the man God had chosen as Israel's future king. She also did the unthinkable: she offered herself as a scapegoat on behalf of a man she knew to be stupid and harsh.

Abigail's wisdom saved not only Nabal and his household but also David's reputation. She reminded David that he was known for leaving vengeance to God, and she encouraged him to enter his kingship in innocence. Her wisdom abrogated David's rash threat. Through Abigail, God showed grace to Nabal's household and to Israel's future king.

Abigail's sacrifice foreshadowed that of another—the Man who would become the scapegoat for all humanity.

Sacrifice marks God's people. Christians live amid hostility, but Jesus told us to respond with obedience to God's Word. When we do, we become instruments of grace in a harsh and foolish world. God furthers His kingdom through His people who live in submission to His will rather than their own, to His reality rather than the world's. Though it sometimes means disregarding our own rights or even putting ourselves in danger, when Christians display God's grace, He brings goodness into places of desolation.

God has promised to set things right and bring about justice for those who believe in Him. For David and Abigail, this meant avengement and reward. God took Nabal's life and brought David and Abigail together in marriage—a union that held the potential to bring wisdom and grace to Israel.

For believers today, God's promise means freedom to be people of wisdom and grace in our world. One day God will set all things right—Jesus will come again, and He will bring justice with Him. Strengthened by that hope, we can be gracious, generous, and hospitable toward all people, even those who insult and deny us.

~*Heather A. Goodman*

THE REST OF THE STORY: Read 1 Samuel 25:1–44.

Do you have a reputation as someone who brings levelhead-edness and a right understanding of God's will to difficult situations? How can you be an instrument of God's grace in adverse circumstances rather than an advocate for your own rights?

"Do not fear, for I will surely show kindness to you for the sake of your father Jonathan, and will restore to you all the land of your grandfather Saul; and you shall eat at my table regularly."

~2 Samuel 9:7

Mephibosheth

Finding Grace in Hiding

In biblical times, tragedy swept across lands regularly. Rulers came to power by blood—familial or shed—and they protected their thrones with fervency. To eliminate threats of revenge, when a king was overthrown, the new king destroyed every trace of the former ruler, including his family.

As the empire of King Saul stood on the verge of obliteration, Saul's family braced themselves. Saul's son, Jonathan, had made a covenant with Israel's next king, David (1 Samuel 18:3), and graciously risked his life to save his best friend (20:1–42). But now, Jonathan could feel the rumblings—not only would he not become king, he and his family were marked. Would David honor their covenant?

When Saul's dynasty met destruction, his entire family fell to the sword . . . except for Jonathan's son Mephibosheth, whose caregiver swept him up to safety. However, in their escape, the caregiver tripped, and the boy plunged into a crippling fall. At only five years old, Mephibosheth had lost his family and the use of his legs; in addition, he had to live in hiding in the desert-like land of *Lo-debar*, which is rendered, "no pasture."

Sometimes life takes everything from us but breath itself. Catastrophes leave us feeling lost, forgotten, and hurt. Maybe you've lost your health. Maybe the loss of a child or mate has devastated you. Poverty, homelessness, disease, death—

tragedy finds us all. But Mephibosheth's story assures us: we're not alone.

In 2 Samuel 9, David, having taken his place as king, remembered his covenant with Jonathan and asked, "Is there yet anyone left of the house of Saul, that I may show him kindness for Jonathan's sake?" (2 Samuel 9:1). The Hebrew word translated "kindness" carries with it the sense of a merciful or gracious act. David wanted to know if there was anyone to whom he could offer grace. He didn't ask for someone fit or deserving or who might give him something in return. He simply asked for *anyone*. And upon learning Jonathan's son was physically disabled, David extended grace to Mephibosheth without hesitation, the same way God gives us grace, seeing our value as His creations regardless of our brokenness (9:7).

David's mercy reminds us that whatever crushes us is part of God's bigger plan. It may not seem so, but that's one reason God gave us stories like Mephibosheth's . . . to remind us that from utter ruin, something beautiful can be born . . . and God's grace is never absent, even when it seems hidden.

~*Colleen Swindoll Thompson*

THE REST OF THE STORY: Read 2 Samuel 9:1–13.

How has God been faithful to you in the past? What crushing struggles are you currently facing? Have you asked God to help you begin to heal through His grace?

_____

_____

_____

_____

_____

_____

_____

_____

_____

_____

_____

_____

_____

_____

_____

_____

_____

"In this matter may the Lord pardon your servant: when my master goes into the house of Rimmon to worship there, and he leans on my hand and I bow myself in the house of Rimmon, when I bow myself in the house of Rimmon, the Lord pardon your servant in this matter." He said to him, "Go in peace."

~ 2 Kings 5:18–19

Naaman

Taking Grace Along for the Journey

When a mother teaches her son how to make his bed, she doesn't expect precision right away. With time, her son will learn to put on the pillowcases and smooth out the wrinkles. But while he learns, a loving mother extends grace and desires obedience, not perfection.

The learning process requires grace. Step by step, babies become toddlers, and miraculously, teenagers become adults. But it doesn't happen all at once. And neither does sanctification. It takes place slowly with time, prayer, and training. Failures and victories mark the road to Christlikeness, and God extends endless grace along the path.

In 2 Kings, we see this kind of grace in action when Naaman, a new believer, asked God's permission to assist his master while he worshiped the idol Rimmon.

Naaman, a valiant warrior and respected leader, commanded the army of Aram. But Naaman was a leper. His skin disease caused him pain day and night. And finally when Naaman had had enough, he sought healing from the God of Israel. After following the prophet Elisha's command to plunge into the Jordan, Naaman came out clean, praising Yahweh.

In response, Naaman determined to turn away from idols and pursue the Lord, but his position required him to assist the king as he worshiped Rimmon. So Naaman asked God to cover this task with grace. Naaman's trip to Israel resulted in a new relationship with God, but Naaman still had to return to his old life in a land filled with false gods and false worship. And God's grace accompanied Naaman every step of the way.

In further pursuit of grace, Naaman asked Elisha for dirt from Israel to take back to Aram. Naaman wanted to exercise his new faith, but he still held on to some pagan ideas. In the ancient Near East, people commonly associated certain gods with certain locations. So Naaman, who likely held this belief, lugged dirt from Israel back to his home country of Aram so that when he worshiped, his knees would touch the soil of God's land. Naaman, though young in his faith, wanted to live as a true believer.

And God's grace met Naaman right where he was.

Think back to your days as a new Christian. Passion for the Christian life might have filled your heart, but sometimes foolishness informed your actions. We often carry pre-conversion baggage on our journeys of sanctification. But slowly, God enables believers to leave those bags behind. When the Holy Spirit begins to conform a Christian to the image of Christ, He doesn't do it all at once—He does it over a lifetime. And just as it did in Naaman's life, God's amazing grace permeates every minute of every day.

~ Malia Rodriguez

THE REST OF THE STORY: Read 2 Kings 5:1–19.

What pre-conversion baggage have you lugged into your Christian life? How has God extended grace to you, and how can you show grace to new Christians?

_____

_____

_____

_____

_____

_____

_____

_____

_____

_____

_____

_____

_____

_____

_____

_____

_____

_____

Joash did what was right in the sight of the LORD all the days of Jehoiada the priest.

~2 Chronicles 24:2

Joash

Depending on People
Rather Than Listening to God

We all need people to influence us. God made us that way.

From the languages we speak to the character we develop—it all begins with those who surround us in our formative years. It starts with our environment, but it shouldn't end there. When it does, it's tragic. That was the case with King Joash. But it doesn't have to be ours.

Joash began life as the only son of King Ahaziah to survive the murderous coup of Athaliah, Joash's grandmother. Rescued as a baby by the grace of God, little Joash grew up safe in the seclusion of the temple under the watchful eye of the godly priest Jehoiada. The boy learned the ways of God for six years while godlessness ruled the land of Judah. When Joash turned seven, Jehoiada had Athaliah executed, and the boy king began his reign. And what a great start he had!

Joash became a man and walked with God. Eventually, the king married and had children. He brought the reforms Judah needed in order to secure God's favor. All was well.

After the priest Jehoiada died, the nation buried him in a place of extreme honor—in the tombs of the kings in the City of David. But in spite of the national honor for the priest, somehow evil had lain dormant in Judah. Jehoiada's death resurrected it.

The officials of Judah approached King Joash and bowed in honor. Then, they influenced for evil the one whom Jehoiada had influenced for good all those years. Joash abandoned the grace of God . . . and served idols. The Lord sent prophets to Joash and urged the king to return. Joash refused and even murdered the son of Jehoiada.

Joash was one who needed someone to tell him what to do. In his youth, by God's grace, that person was godly. But once the priest died, the pendulum in the king's heart swung the other direction. Joash never learned to develop his own convictions. God saved him and taught him in his youth. How gracious! But Joash turned away. How tragic.

However valuable the influence of godly mentors may be in our lives—whether they be parents, pastors, or friends—we need to develop *personal* walks with God. Life demands we cultivate our own resolve to follow the Lord and stand on our own feet.

The people surrounding us as we grew up shaped us, to be sure, for good or for evil. But we each have to decide personally that the Lord is our God and accept His gracious involvement in our lives. As the apostle Paul wrote: "Just as you have always obeyed, not as in my presence only, but now much more in my absence, work out your salvation with fear and trembling" (Philippians 2:12).

When we stand before Him one day, we will stand alone.

~ *Wayne Stiles*

THE REST OF THE STORY: Read 2 Chronicles 22–24.

TAKE IT TO *Heart*

Did your upbringing shape you for good or for bad? What helped you decide to become your own person before God?

_____

_____

_____

_____

_____

_____

_____

_____

_____

_____

_____

_____

_____

_____

_____

_____

_____

_____

_____

_____

Then it happened that night that the angel of the LORD went out and struck 185,000 in the camp of the Assyrians; and when men rose early in the morning, behold, all of them were dead.

~ 2 Kings 19:35

Hezekiah

Unearthing a Mystery

God's people had forgotten. Forgotten the slavery from which they had come. Forgotten who was responsible for their placement in the land. Forgotten to whom they owed their worship.

But along came Hezekiah. And along came grace.

As king of Judah, Hezekiah began to turn the nation around. He sent men to destroy the places of pagan worship throughout Judah, places high on hills and mountains for all to see, places that enticed people to worship gods other than Yahweh, the one true God. And since people worshiped the bronze serpent that Moses had made to rescue the Israelites in the desert, Hezekiah even destroyed that image (Numbers 21:8–9; 2 Kings 18:4).

Hezekiah also beat back his enemies, at least initially. The king led the people to worship their God (2 Chronicles 29). Prosperity came to the land. Ten years of ease descended on Judah.

Then the Assyrian army, a fearsome horde of battle-hardened warriors, descended on the peaceful southern kingdom. Years earlier, Assyria had exiled the Israelites of the northern kingdom and had now come to exact tribute from God's people in the south. Taking the fortified cities of Judah, the Assyrian army eventually surrounded Hezekiah in the capital city of Jerusalem. The king paid what tribute he could by looting the temple of its precious gold and silver treasures—

a moment of weakness that God would eventually overlook. Despite Hezekiah's payment, the Assyrians threatened to overrun Jerusalem as well, seeking to humble a rival nation in one final act of devastating violence (2 Kings 18:13–16, 25).

God had been gracious to Judah through Hezekiah's leadership, and He would be again. In light of continued threats from the Assyrian army, Hezekiah had a simple response: he went to the temple and prayed. Judah's king recognized God's sovereignty, asking directly for deliverance in order to reveal the greatness of God (19:15–19). God chose to use His servant Hezekiah as the means to dispense the grace of deliverance on His people. In response to Hezekiah's prayer, grace came to the people.

But when grace came to Judah, what was the result for Assyria? At times, the "other side" of grace is a terrifying reality for those in disobedience and rebellion. For the massive Assyrian army, that meant death on a devastating scale — 185,000 soldiers — after they continued their campaign against Jerusalem with explicit disrespect and disdain for God and His people. What could have ended in the Assyrians simply heading home in response to a rumor (19:7) instead escalated to destruction due to the Assyrians' rebellious choices (19:8–13). As a result, a wonderful work of grace and deliverance for Judah became unspeakable judgment for the Assyrians . . . and an enduring mystery for us.

~ John Adair

THE REST OF THE STORY: Read 2 Kings 18:1–20:21.

In what ways have you seen the "other side" of grace — grace for some being directly related to judgment for others? What kinds of personal responses have you experienced in those situations?

When he was in distress, he entreated the LORD his God and humbled himself greatly before the God of his fathers.

~ 2 Chronicles 33:12

Manasseh

Responding in Time

Only a child when his father died and left Judah in his hands, Manasseh began reigning at twelve years old. His father had taught the nation to follow the Lord, and its citizens walked upright, until Manasseh came to power. As one of the worst kings of Judah, he destroyed everything good his father had established. Manasseh slaughtered enough innocent blood to fill the city of Jerusalem. He rebuilt idolatrous places of worship, including altars for Baal and Asherah. He even placed carved images of idols in the holy temple of God.

And Manasseh worshiped them. He bowed before these pagan gods. He employed fortune tellers and practiced sorcery and magic. He even sacrificed his own son to the idols. Worst of all, he led the people of Judah into his wicked practices and away from following the Lord. Together, they did more evil than all the nations around.

So the Lord burned with anger.

And Manasseh refused to listen.

We may not slaughter innocent blood, sacrifice our children, or set idols in the temple of God. But we do reach seemingly unredeemable moments. And we silently condemn people we think are unredeemable. They have sinned. We have sinned too. And there is no escape . . . until God provides one.

The notorious Assyrian army captured Manasseh. They bound him with hooks and chains and brought him to Babylon. There, Manasseh suffered. Alone. Away from his kingdom and his idols, Manasseh woke up. He realized he abandoned his father's example and had forsaken the Law of God. In Babylon, Manasseh felt his sin. And it humbled his hardened heart. So he prayed and begged and pleaded with God.

Manasseh humbled himself.

And God listened.

God flooded Manasseh with grace, even with innocent blood on Manasseh's hands and a nation turned to idolatry under his leadership. God listened to this wicked man's humble prayer.

God listened.

Humility always exists as an option. When sin cascades around us and the Enemy binds and chains us, we must choose humility. Those chains may act as instruments of God's grace. They bind until we change.

Can you feel the chains binding you? God may allow harm, suffering, and captivity to come upon you. If He requires of you humbleness, be humble. It's His grace that allows repentance. When you pray, He hears. When you humble yourself, He responds.

With his humbled heart, Manasseh experienced deliverance by God from the Assyrians. The king returned to Jerusalem and reigned until he was sixty-seven. For the remainder of his life, he liberated the land of the idolatry and evil he had fostered. And he will forever be remembered as one of the worst kings in history . . . who humbled himself before it was too late.

~*Andrea Hitefield*

THE REST OF THE STORY: Read 2 Kings 21:1–18; 2 Chronicles 33:1–20.

Are you setting up idols in your life where the Lord should reign? Do you feel like Manasseh, so far away from God that you cannot fathom grace?

_____

_____

_____

_____

_____

_____

_____

_____

_____

_____

_____

_____

_____

_____

_____

_____

_____

"Go, inquire of the LORD for me and the people and all Judah concerning the words of this book that has been found, for great is the wrath of the LORD that burns against us, because our fathers have not listened to the words of this book, to do according to all that is written concerning us."

~ 2 Kings 22:13

Josiah

Cleansing the Land

In the early years of Josiah's reign, pagan worship dominated the landscape of his kingdom. Columns of smoke curled into the sky from idolatrous high places and altars. At these smoldering centers of idol worship, the wayward people burned incense in honor of heavenly bodies, slaughtered horses for the sun at the entrance to God's holy temple, and sacrificed their sons and daughters to the foreign god Molech in the fires of the valley of Hinnom (2 Kings 23:4, 10–11). And *inside* God's temple, the center of worship for all God's people? They filled it not just with idols of Baal, Asherah, and others but also tents pitched for male prostitutes to peddle their wares. The land of Judah under the rule of God's people had never seen worse.

Nothing in Josiah's background suggested he would have had any impulse to change the direction of his kingdom. Assassins ended the life of his father, Amon, after only a two-year reign over Judah. Josiah's grandfather, Manasseh, reigned fifty-five years but was single-handedly responsible for remaking Judah in the image of foreign lands, rather than that of God, who had provided the land. The evil perpetrated by Josiah's fathers left him in a world wholly given to personal impulse, lustful desire, and misdirected worship.

But in a turn that can only be explained by grace, Josiah had an impulse to do some good. He asked a palace official about some damage to the temple. Stones were broken. Wood needed replacing. Josiah saw to it that workmen were hired and the process of restoration begun.

But God had an even greater restoration in mind. The Lord wanted restoration in the lives of those among His people who would respond to Him if given the opportunity. So as the workmen moved into the temple and the high priest, Hilkiah, began to take stock of its contents, he found the book of the Law—the first five books of the Old Testament (2 Kings 22:8). Years of idolatry and rebellion had covered the Law with a thick layer of dust.

When Josiah heard about the book, he immediately had Shaphan, his scribe, read it to him. The contents stirred the tender heart of the king. Josiah then called God's people to the temple so they, too, could hear God's words read to them. A commitment to follow God's commands recorded in the Law soon followed, and Josiah cleansed God's land from all its evil influences (23:3–20).

Grace came to God's people unexpectedly, and they responded with swift and decisive action. Though it wasn't enough to save the whole land from exile, Josiah's good work and soft heart extended the life of a faithful remnant among God's people—a remnant that would remain until the coming of the Messiah.

~John Adair

THE REST OF THE STORY: Read 2 Kings 22:1–23:30.

How has the coming of grace into your own life led you to decisive action and change? Have you witnessed similar movements in the lives of other believers?

_____

_____

_____

_____

_____

_____

_____

_____

_____

_____

_____

_____

_____

_____

_____

_____

_____

"For if you remain silent at this time, relief and deliverance will arise for the Jews from another place and you and your father's house will perish. And who knows whether you have not attained royalty for such a time as this?"

~ Esther 4:14

Esther

Existing for This Moment

One edict had already changed her life, taking her away from her Uncle Mordecai and into the palace—a world of strangers and strange customs. Now, Esther watched as another edict threatened to take the lives of her people.

King Ahasuerus's appointed ruler, Haman, hissed a plan into action: annihilate the Jews. As this edict passed, Mordecai paced through the city wailing. Esther tried to comfort him. He refused. He had only one request—for Esther to go to the king and beg for the Jews' freedom. Esther hesitated. She knew approaching the king uninvited would result in death. But Mordecai reminded her of her heritage and admonished her with an unanswerable question, "Who knows whether you have not attained royalty for such a time as this?"(Esther 4:14).

Surely, Esther contemplated that question throughout the night. Though the threat of death remained, Esther knew what she had to do. She begged her people to fast with her until the day she stood in the inner court of the king's palace.

The chamber echoed as Esther waited. Days of anticipation had led to the moment. And whether she lived or died had little impact on her approach. Esther existed for this moment. She was created for such a time as this.

Her heart thundered.

For such a time as this . . .

Each step resounded off the columns.

For such a time as this . . .

She placed her trembling foot down once more and waited.

For such a time . . .

Mordecai's admonishment to Esther rings true for us today. Often, our fear brings hesitation. Worry floods our minds as we overanalyze every decision. Undoubtedly, Esther's mind flooded too. But to be obedient, she could not wait for fear to disappear. Esther approached the king expecting death but found his delight instead. God had a plan, and He used Esther as His instrument. Through her boldness, God extended grace to the Jewish nation.

Like Esther, we have the choice to accept or reject the opportunity to allow God's grace to pour through us. But even when we say no, His grace doesn't stop. God will use anyone and any means to fulfill His purpose. If Esther had said no, God would have used someone else. And if you or I say no, He will use someone else.

But He didn't choose someone other than Esther. He chose her. And He has chosen us. In spite of fear, we can trust that His plans are beyond our understanding. We can let Him show us our place in them. And, when we're willing, we can let His grace flow through us to those who desperately need it.

~Andrea Hitefield

THE REST OF THE STORY: Read Esther 7–9.

When your circumstances do not align with the plans you have for your life, do you trust that you were created "for such a time as this"? Seeing the grace of God through another often helps us see the grace of God in our own lives. In what ways has God poured grace through you? How can you allow a deeper flow of grace?

"Where now is my hope?

And who regards my hope?

Will it go down with me to Sheol?

Shall we together go down into the dust?"

~Job 17:15–16

Needing Grace in the Fog

Job had reached absolute rock bottom. Death seemed his only recourse, his one and only refuge of relief.

You know what he was missing? What only grace could bring him. Hope. He received no grace from anybody around him, and that left him with no hope. He had nobody to reassure him . . . nobody to affirm him. He was totally confused. He couldn't find his way.

A thick blanket of fog was rolling into Job's life, just like in our lives. On this earth, nobody "lives happily ever after." That line is a huge fairytale. You're living in a dream if you're waiting for it. That's why we need grace.

Marriage doesn't get easier; it gets harder. We need grace to keep it together. Work doesn't get easier; it gets more complicated. We need grace to stay diligent on the job. Childrearing doesn't get easier. You who have one-, two-, three-year-olds— you think you've got it tough? Wait until they're fourteen. Or eighteen. Talk about needing grace! And, hey—if you thought you were fat when you got married, take a glance in a full-length mirror. We even need *grace* as we gain weight!

Everything gets harder.

We need *grace* to go on. Grace and more grace. We need *grace* to relate, *grace* to drive, *grace* to stay positive, *grace* to keep a church in unity, *grace* to be good neighbors. We need *grace* as we get older. We need *grace* when times are good. We need *grace* when that old fog rolls in and there's nothing under our feet but mess and mud.

That's where Job was when his friends found him. And what did they do? They offered accusations, insults, and condemnation . . . just about everything except grace. With each encounter, Job sunk deeper. Let's never forget the flip side of what Job's "comforters" modeled: when folks are out of hope, don't kick them, don't criticize them, and don't hold them under. *Administer grace!*

Thankfully, though Job couldn't see it at first, God's grace was active in his life, even when he hit bottom. If we called the shots, we would have relieved Job five minutes after he lost everything. We would've brought his kids back to life. We would've immediately replaced everything, and then we would have dealt with those sorry people who called themselves his friends!

But you know what? No one would ever grow up and cultivate maturity under that kind of treatment. God knows that. That's why the fog is God's grace too.

Even in the fog, grace will lead us home. Dear, beat-up Job was so miserable he wasn't even thinking beyond the grave. We understand. But we also know there is a tomorrow, and by God's grace, there is a home beyond. There was for Job too, but he couldn't see it. The fog was too thick.

Let's remember that when the fog rolls into our lives.

~ *Charles R. Swindoll*

THE REST OF THE STORY: Read Job 17; 42:7–9.

Have tough circumstances rolled into your life like a fog that has blinded you to the truth beyond the pain? How can Job's limited vision in his trials help you gain a broader perspective and find hope and grace in your own struggles?

"Holy, Holy, Holy, is the LORD of hosts,

The whole earth is full of His glory."

And the foundations of the thresholds trembled at the voice of him who called out, while the temple was filling with smoke.

Then I said,

"Woe is me, for I am ruined!"

~ Isaiah 6:3–5

Isaiah

Finding Ruin and Redemption at the Throne of God

The young prophet was exposed. In a spectacular vision, he was thrust beyond earthly bonds into a heavenly dimension. At the throne of God, Isaiah stood ashamed and trembling.

Rarely do humans experience paralyzing awe — awe like the heart-stopping wonder that overwhelms space explorers as they pass the earth's atmosphere into shimmering starlight or the helpless trembling that overtakes the person cowering under a blasting monsoon. This is the kind of awe Isaiah knew when he saw the sovereign Lord "sitting on a throne, lofty and exalted" (Isaiah 6:1).

Smoke filled the temple. The sonic boom of angels' voices shook the door frames. The Creator overshadowed the young prophet, a sprig of grass bowed in the eye of a hurricane. Bracing himself in the presence of perfect moral purity and absolute power, Isaiah said, "Woe is me, for I am ruined!" (6:5).

With his own eyes on the Holy One of Israel, the prophet was confronted with the outrage of his sin and of Israel's sin, the frightful purity of God's holiness, and the crush of condemnation. One touch from the burning coal that the heavenly messenger held completely removed Isaiah's guilt, and the angel announced, "Your sin is forgiven." This grand vision of

God's grace prepared the prophet to carry words of impending woe and momentous deliverance not only to Israel but to the whole world.

Strengthened by God's tangible grace, Isaiah, whose name means "God saves," entered a time of great uncertainty. For sixty years, God used Isaiah's brush to paint a vast mural in two parts captured in the book that bears his name. One half displays Israel's judgment through Assyria and future captivity in Babylon (chapters 1 to 39). The other half pictures salvation, comfort, and grace brought to Israel through purifying, fiery trials and, ultimately, the Suffering Servant (chapters 40 to 66). Isaiah's prophecies have enormous range, from the judgments of his time to the coming Messiah and all the way to the eternal kingdom.

No amount of religious work, denial, or self-congratulations can remove our sin. When God gives us the vision to see clearly, like Isaiah, we recognize that we are doomed. Through Christ and His completed suffering for our sin, the Holy One declares, *It is finished. Your guilt is removed, and your sins are forgiven.* We are exposed like Isaiah and purified by Christ. What's more, God sends us into the world. What grace! What wonder and awe that the Savior lifts us from sin-wrecked doom to deployment in sanctified service of the living God. When the Sovereign Master asks, "Whom shall I send, and who will go for Us?" it's the pure grace of the Prince of Peace that strengthens us to say, "Here am I. Send me!" (Isaiah 6:8).

~*Brian Leicht*

THE REST OF THE STORY: Read Isaiah 6:1–8; 9:2–7.

Can you recall a time in your life when you experienced conviction for sin and the relief of God's grace? Why is knowing God's grace in a personal way so essential to your own spiritual growth and ministry?

So they pulled Jeremiah up with the ropes and lifted him out of the cistern, and Jeremiah stayed in the court of the guardhouse.

~Jeremiah 38:13

Jeremiah

Escaping the Morass

Outside the walls of Jerusalem, the Babylonian army sat arrayed in terrible splendor. For eighteen interminable months, its siege of Judah's capital advanced with the grim certainty of a funeral procession. Soon, the long-sought land of the Israelites would belong to Babylon (2 Kings 25:1–4).

Inside the walls of Jerusalem, God's people staved off starvation by hoarding every crust of bread and cherishing every drop of water. They hoped for help from Egypt, but it would not come. The city walls closed in on them like a coffin's lid.

Even God's prophet Jeremiah, surrounded by death and refuse, stalked the stinking streets of Jerusalem offering only words of judgment, predictions that the Babylonians would capture and burn the city (Jeremiah 37:8). Where was victory? When would the Lord overcome the evil invaders? How were God's chosen people to survive this onslaught? God had abandoned His people to their own devices and taken His grace with Him.

Or so it seemed.

At least one resident of Jerusalem remained faithful. That prophet of doom, Jeremiah, accurately delivered the words of the Lord and ended up suffering even greater indignities than his neighbors. Those same neighbors turned on Jeremiah, believing him to be secretly serving the Babylonian cause

(Jeremiah 37:13). After Jeremiah's arrest, Zedekiah, a hypo-critical puppet king installed by Babylon's emperor, summoned Jeremiah to the palace and sought a word of deliverance from the Lord. But when Jeremiah had only words of judgment, Zedekiah kept the prophet captive without cause (37:17, 21).

Undeterred, Jeremiah continued to preach from the busy courtyard where the king's guard kept him. His doomsday message eventually enraged a group of palace officials. They believed Jeremiah's negativity was hurting morale in the besieged city, so they received permission to execute him. They lowered the prophet into an empty cistern—a pit for holding water—leaving him as much as thirty feet below the surface to die. What should have held the means for life was instead becoming a tomb.

Sinking in mud at the bottom of the cistern with no means of escape and the city out of bread, Jeremiah would have surely died alone in the dark (38:6–9). But God had not abandoned His faithful servant.

God sent grace in the form of a foreigner, an Ethiopian named Ebed-melech, who took it upon himself to petition the king for Jeremiah's release. Ebed-melech threw God's prophet a lifeline of dirty rags and worn-out clothes, bringing him back to light and life (38:11–13).

People seeking to do us evil—hypocrites telling us one thing and doing another—times of loneliness and darkness . . . we have all travelled these valleys that Jeremiah knew well. Yet, God's grace remains—even if we, like Jeremiah, cannot see it until it's upon us.

~John Adair

THE REST OF THE STORY: Read Jeremiah 37:1–39:12.

What aspect of grace in Jeremiah's story stands out to you? Why? How has God brought His grace upon you in a dark time?

_____

_____

_____

_____

_____

_____

_____

_____

_____

_____

_____

_____

_____

_____

_____

_____

_____

_____

_____

"But you, are you seeking great things for yourself? Do not seek them; for behold, I am going to bring disaster on all flesh," declares the LORD, "but I will give your life to you as booty in all the places where you may go."

~Jeremiah 45:5

Baruch

Finding Grace in Life

Our culture taunts us with hopes of comfort and ease, promising we can get rich quick, live "the good life," and evade responsibility. But Christ invites us to journey with Him on the narrow road that leads to eternal life. This hard path requires self-denial and God-focused obedience—not because the Lord loves suffering but because He wants us to depend on Him, cling to Him, and love Him. He wants a relationship with us. He wants what will ultimately benefit us—*Him*! The Lord wants us to experience His grace in the midst of suffering.

The book of Jeremiah records God's words of judgment and restoration to His people, many of whom suffered in Babylonian exile because of their disobedience. In Jerusalem, Jeremiah and Baruch languished with the few remaining Jews. The path of these two men zigzagged through the devastated streets of Jerusalem, as they faithfully proclaimed God's message to His people. The Lord entrusted them with a mighty task—a task both difficult and depressing—and He preserved their lives every day. With each step on the ruined roads of Jerusalem, they experienced God's grace.

But one day, weary under his heavy load of grief, Baruch complained: "Ah, woe is me! For the LORD has added sorrow to my pain; I am weary with my groaning and have found no rest" (Jeremiah 45:3). Baruch, who endured persecution as

Jeremiah's scribe, mourned because Jerusalem lay desolate and God's people suffered in exile.

The Lord responded to Baruch's complaint with grace, reminding the scribe that while many of God's people had died because of their disobedience, He had preserved Baruch's life. With each new day, God gave Baruch the grace he needed to obey His call.

Baruch, whose name means "blessed," came from a noble family and may have expected a life of wealth and prominence. But God's path of persecution produced for Baruch a better reward. While God's judgment led to death among the Jews, He graciously preserved Baruch's life so that he could serve God, depend on Him daily, and store up eternal treasure.

Often, God's grace shines brightest in the midst of trials that highlight our need for Him. In comfort and ease, we're tempted to disregard God and rely on ourselves; we forget to look for and be thankful for grace. God's words to Baruch remind us that life, even when accompanied by suffering, is a gracious gift. Each day presents a new chance to participate in God's plan of redemption. The Lord showed grace by sparing Baruch's life. And the difficult road God paved for the scribe deepened his faith and strengthened his bond with his Creator, revealing God's grace all the more.

~ *Malia Rodriguez*

THE REST OF THE STORY: Read Jeremiah 36:1–8; 45.

How do you define grace—as blessing, prosperity, or the opportunity to serve God? Do you prefer comfort over trials, even if those trials will bring you closer to God?

_____

_____

_____

_____

_____

_____

_____

_____

_____

_____

_____

_____

_____

_____

_____

_____

_____

"The king reflected and said, 'Is this not Babylon the great, which I myself have built as a royal residence by the might of my power and for the glory of my majesty?'"

~ Daniel 4:30

Nebuchadnezzar

Dreaming of Grace

Nebuchadnezzar awoke drenched. He grabbed his chest. He couldn't catch his breath. His heart pounded in his temples—thump, thump. Surely others could hear its echo against the stone walls. Fear flooded his mind. What did his nightmare mean?

He called the magicians and astrologers. But they didn't understand what the massive tree symbolized, nor why an angelic being chopped it down. These "wise" men couldn't comprehend how a tree could receive an animal's mind. Frustrated, the king sent them away.

Then Nebuchadnezzar remembered: Daniel's God could reveal dreams.

As Daniel interpreted, the king had a gnawing sense that the dream was about him. But *why* did the angel fell the powerful tree, scatter its fruit, and shoo away the animals? And *who* sent the angel? Only a God who rules over the angels, trees, beasts, and the earth could give a tree the mind of an ox. Trees don't have brains. Again he realized, "I am that tree."

The king's head fell back on his pillow. He remembered that God had given him several chances to acknowledge Yahweh as the true King. But Nebuchadnezzar hadn't.

Years earlier, God had graciously revealed His sovereignty to Nebuchadnezzar. In a dream of a huge, metal and clay statue, the Lord disclosed to the king five world empires: Babylon, Medo-Persia, Greece, Rome, and God's eternal kingdom. The Lord alone had the power to establish kingdoms and destroy them. But awe-struck Nebuchadnezzar eventually forgot God's message and again became enthralled with his own dominion.

God extended him grace again. Nebuchadnezzar had sentenced three Hebrew administrators to death for refusing to worship a statue of his god. But the Lord revealed His power to protect His servants. As the king sat down to watch the Hebrews burn in his furnace, he saw them walking with an angelic being through the flames, unharmed and unshackled. Surely a God with authority over fire, who commanded angels to carry out His plans, deserved worship! But the memory of God's grace faded, and Nebuchadnezzar again basked in his own glory.

The king's heart still pounded; sweat streamed down his forehead. The Babylonian ruler recalled these chances he had missed . . . and cringed. This time God had threatened to make Nebuchadnezzar live as a beast for seven years if he didn't kneel.

Throughout our lives, God sends us opportunities to accept His grace. When we reject them, His grace may extend to consequences that will get our attention and lead to a change in our hearts. Nebuchadnezzar knew such grace. Seven years after his nightmare became reality, the king knelt before Yahweh. Finally, Nebuchadnezzar responded wholeheartedly to God's sovereign grace. The once-prideful ruler came to his senses, turned his eyes toward heaven, and "blessed the Most High and praised and honored Him who lives forever" (Daniel 4:34).

~ *Malia Rodriguez*

THE REST OF THE STORY: Read Daniel 2–4.

In what areas of your life have you refused to bow to God? What will it take to get you on your knees?

_____

_____

_____

_____

_____

_____

_____

_____

_____

_____

_____

_____

_____

_____

_____

_____

_____

_____

Then the LORD said to me, "Go again, love a woman who is loved by her husband, yet an adulteress, even as the LORD loves the sons of Israel, though they turn to other gods and love raisin cakes."

~Hosea 3:1

Giving Grace to the Graceless

On the eve of their wedding, they looked forward to their future. They dreamt of kids, a house, and lifelong love. Sure, they expected trials, but they believed their marriage would weather the storms. They had no idea how severe the tempests would get.

That's the story in the book of Hosea. . . . That's the story of Israel and her Husband.

With Jeroboam in power, Israel enjoyed prosperity and ease. But with affluence often comes moral decline. As God's chosen people climbed the mountain of fortune, they abandoned Him and tumbled down the other side. They left their heavenly Husband to engage in spiritual prostitution.

God tried to woo His people back through the prophet Hosea, who called Israel to repentance to no avail. So God gave them a living illustration of their betrayal: He arranged a marriage between Hosea and a woman who would eventually break his heart.

Hosea proposed to Gomer, and she said yes. Their marriage started well, but it went south after they had kids. The couple had two sons: Jezreel, the name of the city where Jehu killed Ahab's household, and Lo-ruhamah, which means "no compassion." They also had a daughter, Lo-ammi—"not my people." These little ones reminded the Israelites of the cost of their betrayal. He would withhold compassion until they returned to Him with repentance.

One day, the unthinkable happened. Hosea woke up and Gomer was gone. She had abandoned her husband and their children to pursue other men.

Hosea's pain resonated with God. The wife who had once loved Him had left Him for Baal.

Eventually, Gomer returned, and Hosea welcomed her back with open arms. Israel has not yet returned to her Husband never to leave again . . . but one day, she will.

God has promised to reunite His divided people in their land. Even though they turned their backs, God has promised to show grace. He made an eternal covenant with Abraham, and He intends to keep it! One day, Israel will return to God, and He will welcome them with open arms. They will be His people, and He will be their God!

Have you experienced God's amazing grace? Just as Hosea extended grace to Gomer and accepted her back, God accepts all who turn to Him through faith in His Son. If you've put your trust in Jesus Christ, God has made you His child. You can't do anything to diminish His love or overshadow His grace. Thank God for loving you, no matter how many times you fail. Thank Him for His amazing grace.

~ *Malia Rodriguez*

THE REST OF THE STORY: Read the book of Hosea.

TAKE IT TO *Heart*

How do you feel when your loved ones fail you? How does God feel when we don't obey Him? Do you believe that God's grace outweighs your sin?

He said to them, "Pick me up and throw me into the sea. Then the sea will become calm for you, for I know that on account of me this great storm has come upon you." . . . So they picked up Jonah, threw him into the sea, and the sea stopped its raging.

~Jonah 1:12, 15

Jonah

Walking the Plank

Jonah sinned against the Lord by disobeying God's direct command to "cry against" the notoriously wicked citizens of Nineveh (Jonah 1:2). Rather than traveling east to the great city of Nineveh — believed to be in what is modern-day Iraq — Jonah set sail on a ship headed the opposite direction, west toward the coastal city of Tarshish — believed to be in what is now Spain. Jonah acted with such blatant disobedience because he feared a confrontation with the cruel and brutal citizens of Nineveh.

But God did not (and still does not) take kindly to being disobeyed, and He proved this point by hurling Jonah's Tarshish-bound boat to and fro in a stormy Mediterranean Sea. After a time of confusion and dismay over the cause of the typhoon, the boat's crew finally deduced the reason for the fell storm: a sinner was among them, and that sinner was Jonah. To appease Jonah's angry God, they dispatched Jonah to the roiling sea. The storm immediately calmed.

God showed mercy and grace to Jonah after he was thrown overboard — not just once but many times. God spared Jonah from drowning by sending a big fish to swallow him. God gave Jonah three days in the belly of that fish to come to his senses and repent. God caused the big fish to spit up Jonah on the shore. God safely allowed Jonah to proclaim the divine decree against Nineveh. And the list goes on.

East, west, north, south . . . like the directions of a compass, God—through His Word, through our prayers, and through the wisdom of godly people—charts for us the bearing we should take. Whether or not we obey and go in His direction is up to us. But if we choose to go our own direction, one way or another, our journey will become storm-tossed. When that happens, it's not God being vindictive or vengeful in response to our disobedience. It's God showing His children great, great mercy . . . it's God telling us to change course, for the direction He wants us to go is the right and *best* direction. His course will not always be smooth sailing. He never claims it will be, but His course is infinitely better than not going His way (Isaiah 48:17; 2 Corinthians 2:14).

The moral to Jonah's story? Don't jeopardize God's great grace through disobedience. Just do what He wants you to do in the first place . . . otherwise, in addition to the pain you and others will receive by your own actions, you'll reek of fish!

~Jim Craft

THE REST OF THE STORY: Read Jonah 1:1–4:11.

Have you ever run away from God when He commanded you to do something? Are you afraid of doing what He wants you to do now? Why?

How to Begin a Relationship with God

Salvation in Jesus Christ comes to us by one avenue and one avenue only: the grace of God. Without His empowering and transforming grace, we would all be lost in the pursuit of fulfilling our selfish desires and acting out our wicked behavior. However, by grace and through faith in the sacrifice of His Son, Jesus, God has allowed us the privilege of a life transformed. And as recipients of grace, God's people seek to share that grace with others.

The Bible marks the path to salvation through God's grace with four essential truths. Let's look at each truth in detail.

Our Spiritual Condition: Totally Depraved

The first truth is rather personal. One look in the mirror of Scripture, and our human condition becomes painfully clear:

> "There is none righteous, not even one;
> There is none who understands,
> There is none who seeks for God;
> All have turned aside, together they have
>   become useless;
> There is none who does good,
> There is not even one." (Romans 3:10–12)

We are all sinners through and through—totally depraved. Now, that doesn't mean we've committed every atrocity known to humankind. We're not as *bad* as we can be, just as *bad off* as we can be. Sin colors all our thoughts, motives, words, and actions.

If you've been around a while, you likely already believe it. Look around. Everything around us bears the smudge marks of our sinful nature. Despite our best efforts to create a perfect world, crime statistics continue to soar, divorce rates keep climbing, and families keep crumbling.

Something has gone terribly wrong in our society and in ourselves—something deadly. Contrary to how the world would repackage it, "me-first" living doesn't equal rugged individuality and freedom; it equals death. As Paul said in his letter to the Romans, "The wages of sin is death" (Romans 6:23)—our spiritual and physical death that comes from God's righteous judgment of our sin, along with all of the emotional and practical effects of this separation that we experience on a daily basis. This brings us to the second marker: God's character.

God's Character: Infinitely Holy

How can God judge us for a sinful state we were born into? Our total depravity is only half the answer. The other half is God's infinite holiness.

The fact that we know things are not as they should be points us to a standard of goodness beyond ourselves. Our sense of injustice in life on this side of eternity implies a perfect standard of justice beyond our reality. That standard and source is God Himself. And God's standard of holiness contrasts starkly with our sinful condition.

Scripture says that "God is Light, and in Him there is no darkness at all" (1 John 1:5). God is absolutely holy—which creates a problem for us. If He is so pure, how can we who are so impure relate to Him?

Perhaps we could try being better people, try to tilt the balance in favor of our good deeds, or seek out methods for self-improvement. Throughout history, people have attempted to live up to God's standard by keeping the Ten Commandments or living by their own code of ethics. Unfortunately, no one can come close to satisfying the demands of God's law. Romans 3:20 says, "By the works of the Law no flesh will be justified in His sight; for through the Law comes the knowledge of sin."

Our Need: A Substitute

So here we are, sinners by nature and sinners by choice, trying to pull ourselves up by our own bootstraps to attain a relationship with our holy Creator. But every time we try, we fall flat on our faces. We can't live a good enough life to make up for our sin, because God's standard isn't "good enough"—it's *perfection*. And we can't make amends for the offense our sin has created without dying for it.

Who can get us out of this mess?

If someone could live perfectly, honoring God's law, and would bear sin's death penalty for us—in our place—then we would be saved from our predicament. But is there such a person? Thankfully, yes!

Meet your substitute—*Jesus Christ*. He is the One who took death's place for you!

[God] made [Jesus Christ] who knew no
sin to be sin on our behalf, so that we might
become the righteousness of God in Him.
(2 Corinthians 5:21)

God's Provision: A Savior

God rescued us by sending His Son, Jesus, to die on the cross
for our sins (1 John 4:9–10). Jesus was fully human and fully
divine (John 1:1, 18), a truth that ensures His understanding of
our weaknesses, His power to forgive, and His ability to bridge
the gap between God and us (Romans 5:6–11). In short, we are
"justified as a gift by His grace through the redemption which
is in Christ Jesus" (Romans 3:24). Two words in this verse bear
further explanation: *justified* and *redemption*.

Justification is God's act of mercy, in which He declares righteous the believing sinners while we are still in our sinning state.
Justification doesn't mean that God *makes* us righteous, so that
we never sin again, rather that He *declares* us righteous—much
like a judge pardons a guilty criminal. Because Jesus took our
sin upon Himself and suffered our judgment on the cross, God
forgives our debt and proclaims us PARDONED.

Redemption is Christ's act of paying the complete price to
release us from sin's bondage. God sent His Son to bear His wrath
for all of our sins—past, present, and future (Romans 3:24–26;
2 Corinthians 5:21). In humble obedience, Christ willingly
endured the shame of the cross for our sake (Mark 10:45;
Romans 5:6–8; Philippians 2:8). Christ's death satisfied God's
righteous demands. He no longer holds our sins against us,
because His own Son paid the penalty for them. We are freed
from the slave market of sin, never to be enslaved again!

Placing Your Faith in Christ

These four truths describe how God has provided a way to Himself through Jesus Christ. Because the price has been paid in full by God, we must respond to His free gift of eternal life in total faith and confidence in Him to save us. We must step forward into the relationship with God that He has prepared for us—not by doing good works or by being a good person, but by coming to Him just as we are and accepting His justification and redemption by faith.

> For by grace you have been saved through
> faith; and that not of yourselves, it is the gift of
> God; not as a result of works, so that no one
> may boast. (Ephesians 2:8–9)

We accept God's gift of salvation simply by placing our faith in Christ alone for the forgiveness of our sins. Would you like to enter a relationship with your Creator by trusting in Christ as your Savior? If so, here's a simple prayer you can use to express your faith:

> *Dear God,*
>
> *I know that my sin has put a barrier between You and me. Thank You for sending Your Son, Jesus, to die in my place. I trust in Jesus alone to forgive my sins, and I accept His gift of eternal life. I ask Jesus to be my personal Savior and the Lord of my life. Thank You. In Jesus's name, amen.*

If you've prayed this prayer or one like it and you wish to find out more about knowing God and His plan for you in the Bible, contact us at Insight for Living Ministries. Our contact information is on the following pages.

We Are Here for You

If you desire to find out more about knowing God and His plan for you in the Bible, contact us. Insight for Living Ministries provides staff pastors who are available for free written correspondence or phone consultation. These seminary-trained and seasoned counselors have years of experience and are well-qualified guides for your spiritual journey.

Please feel welcome to contact your regional office by using the information below:

United States

Insight for Living
Biblical Counseling Department
Post Office Box 269000
Plano, Texas 75026-9000
USA
972-473-5097, Monday through Friday,
8:00 a.m.–5:00 p.m. central time
www.insight.org/contactapastor

Canada

Insight for Living Canada
Biblical Counseling Department
PO Box 8 Stn A
Abbotsford BC   V2T 6Z4
CANADA
1-800-663-7639
info@insightforliving.ca

Australia, New Zealand, and South Pacific

Insight for Living Australia
Pastoral Care
Post Office Box 443
Boronia, VIC 3155
AUSTRALIA
1300 467 444

United Kingdom and Europe

Insight for Living United Kingdom
Pastoral Care
PO Box 553
Dorking
RH4 9EU
UNITED KINGDOM
0800 787 9364
+44 (0)1306 640156
pastoralcare@insightforliving.org.uk

Resources for Probing Further

We have seen grace throughout the Old Testament, impacting lives as God worked out His plan on earth—a plan that is still in process. Grace doesn't exist only in the Bible; God continues to use it in our world and in our lives today. As you seek to further your study of grace, we recommend the following resources. Of course, we cannot always endorse everything a writer or ministry says, so we encourage you to approach these and all other resources outside the Bible with wisdom and discernment.

Bridges, Jerry. *Transforming Grace: Living Confidently in God's Unfailing Love*. Colorado Springs: NavPress, 2008.

Chafer, Lewis Sperry. *Grace: An Exposition of God's Marvelous Gift*. Grand Rapids: Kregel, 1995.

Manning, Brennan. *Abba's Child: The Cry of the Heart for Intimate Belonging*. Colorado Springs: NavPress, 2002.

Manning, Brennan. *The Ragamuffin Gospel*. Sisters: Ore.: Multnomah, 2005.

McVey, Steve. *Grace Walk: What You've Always Wanted in the Christian Life*. Eugene, Ore.: Harvest House, 1995.

Smedes, Lewis B. *Shame and Grace: Healing the Shame We Don't Deserve*. New York: HarperCollins, 1994.

Walvoord, John F. and Roy B. Zuck. *The Bible Knowledge Commentary: An Exposition of the Scriptures by Dallas Seminary Faculty*. Old Testament ed. Wheaton, Ill.: Victor Books, 1986.

Wiersbe, Warren W. *The Wiersbe Bible Commentary: The Complete Old Testament in One Volume*. Colorado Springs: David C. Cook, 2007.

Yancey, Phillip. *What's So Amazing About Grace?* Grand Rapids: Zondervan, 2002.

About the Writers

Charles R. Swindoll

Charles R. Swindoll has devoted his life to the accurate, practical teaching and application of God's Word and His grace. A pastor at heart, Chuck has served as senior pastor to congregations in Texas, Massachusetts, and California. Since 1998, he has served as the founder and senior pastor-teacher of Stonebriar Community Church in Frisco, Texas, but Chuck's listening audience extends far beyond a local church body. As a leading program in Christian broadcasting since 1979, *Insight for Living* airs in major Christian radio markets around the world, reaching people groups in languages they can understand. Chuck's extensive writing ministry has also served the body of Christ worldwide and his leadership as president and now chancellor of Dallas Theological Seminary has helped prepare and equip a new generation for ministry. Chuck and Cynthia, his partner in life and ministry, have four grown children, ten grandchildren, and two great-grandchildren.

John Adair
Th.M., Ph.D., Dallas Theological Seminary

John received his bachelor's degree from Criswell College and his master of theology degree from Dallas Theological Seminary, where he also completed his Ph.D. in Historical Theology. He serves as a writer in the Creative Ministries Department of

Insight for Living. John, his wife, Laura, and their three children reside in Frisco, Texas.

Terry Boyle
Th.M., Ph.D., Dallas Theological Seminary

Terry holds a master of theology degree in Pastoral Ministries and a doctor of philosophy in Biblical Studies from Dallas Theological Seminary. In his role as pastor for Insight for Living United Kingdom, Terry preaches, teaches, and trains other leaders at churches throughout the United Kingdom. He also helps listeners with their theological questions and personal problems. Terry has been married to Rosie, a surgical nurse, for thirty years, and they have three grown children.

Jim Craft
M.A., English, Mississippi College

Jim received his master of arts degree in English from Mississippi College and is currently pursuing a certificate of biblical and theological studies at Dallas Theological Seminary. Jim has served in the Creative Ministries Department at Insight for Living since 2005, where he has the privilege of reading and editing the biblically illumined works of Chuck Swindoll and the Insight for Living team. Jim and his wife, Amber, live in Dallas, Texas.

Heather A. Goodman
Th.M., Dallas Theological Seminary

Heather holds a bachelor's degree from Baylor University and a master of theology degree with an emphasis in Cross-cultural Ministries from Dallas Theological Seminary. Her short stories and articles have appeared in Christian journals and magazines, including *Ruminate Magazine*, *Relief*, and *The High Calling*. She has also written faith-based films, which have been produced for festivals and churches. Heather lives in Plano, Texas, with her husband and two children.

Kimberlee Hertzer
M.A., Christian Education, Dallas Theological Seminary

Kimberlee received a bachelor's degree from Pensacola Christian College and a master of arts degree in Christian Education from Dallas Theological Seminary. She served in the Biblical Counseling Department at Insight for Living, where she responded, through writing and counseling, to women's needs for spiritual direction. Kimberlee's ministry also extends into Christian schools and intercity programs. She and her husband, Chris, live in Plano, Texas, with their two children.

Andrea Hitefield
M.A., Media and Communication, Dallas Theological Seminary

Andrea holds a bachelor's degree from Moody Bible Institute and a master of arts degree in Media and Communication from Dallas Theological Seminary. While pursuing her master's degree, Andrea completed an internship at Insight for Living, where she was mentored by the writing and editing team. Andrea serves as the freshman grade director at Irving Bible Church and currently lives in Dallas, Texas.

Brian Leicht
Th.M., Dallas Theological Seminary

Brian received a master of theology degree in Pastoral Ministries from Dallas Theological Seminary. As director of the Biblical Counseling team at Insight for Living, he provides biblical guidance to listeners through written and verbal correspondence. He has also pastored in single adult, marriage reconciliation, and missions ministries for twenty years. Brian also holds a master's degree in Trumpet Performance, and he, his wife,

Bonnie, and their three sons enjoy participating in worship ministry and local theatre.

Malia Rodriguez
Th.M., Dallas Theological Seminary

Malia received her master of theology degree in Systematic Theology from Dallas Theological Seminary. She now serves as a writer in the Creative Ministries Department of Insight for Living, where she is able to merge her love of theology with her gift for words. Malia and her husband, Matt, who is also a graduate of Dallas Theological Seminary, live in the Dallas area with their newborn son.

Wayne Stiles
Th.M., D.Min., Dallas Theological Seminary

Wayne received his master of theology in Pastoral Ministries and doctor of ministry in Biblical Geography from Dallas Theological Seminary. In 2005, after serving in the pastorate for fourteen years, Wayne joined the staff at Insight for Living, where he leads and labors alongside a team of writers, editors, and pastors as the executive vice president and chief content officer. Wayne and his wife, Cathy, live in Aubrey, Texas, and have two daughters in college.

Colleen Swindoll Thompson
B.A., Communication, Trinity International University

Colleen holds a bachelor of arts degree in Communication from Trinity International University and serves as the director of Special Needs Ministries at Insight for Living. From the personal challenges of raising a child with disabilities (her son Jonathan), Colleen offers help, hope, and a good dose of humor through speaking, writing, and counseling those affected by disability. Colleen and her husband, Toban, have five children and reside in Frisco, Texas.

Ordering Information

If you would like to order additional copies of *Glimpses of Grace: 30 Reflections on Old Testament Lives* or order other Insight for Living Ministries resources, please contact the office that serves you.

United States

Insight for Living
Post Office Box 269000
Plano, Texas 75026-9000
USA
1-800-772-8888
Monday through Friday
7:00 a.m.–7:00 p.m. central time
www.insight.org
www.insightworld.org

Canada

Insight for Living Canada
PO Box 8 Stn A
Abbotsford BC V2T 6Z4
CANADA
1-800-663-7639
www.insightforliving.ca

Australia, New Zealand, and South Pacific

Insight for Living Australia
Post Office Box 443
Boronia, VIC 3155
AUSTRALIA
1300 467 444
www.insight.asn.au

United Kingdom and Europe

Insight for Living United Kingdom
PO Box 553
Dorking
RH4 9EU
UNITED KINGDOM
0800 787 9364
www.insightforliving.org.uk

Other International Locations

International constituents may contact the U.S. office through our Web site (www.insightworld.org), mail queries, or by calling +1-972-473-5136.